ARIEL

Kendrick Ashton Sims

FIRST PUBLISHED 2019

PRINTED IN THE UNITED STATES OF AMERICA

BOOKS BY KENDRICK ASHTON SIMS

2018

The Bully
Lazar & Jingles with Bunson in Holiday Gifts
Lazar & Jingles w/Bunson in Mirrors in Strange Places

2019

Lazar & Jingles with Bunson in Stars Cease to Shine
Mr. Wolfy Goes to the Vet
Cooper Corner
Ariel

It's been over four years since little Ariel first came through my front door. All I can say is that she is still as much my little princess now as she was four years ago. She's still my little girl. Time may pass and I may grow older, but Ariel is still my constant companion. Always by my side purring, sleeping or cuddling.

This little book is but a poem to show one persons appreciation of their furrever friend. I can only hope my words can demonstrate what a wonderful friend she is. For Ariel is the best.

Kendrick,
December 2019

Oh new home, where can I be?

Dare I rise? Oh! What shall I see?

New sights so bright! There's much to explore.

Strange eyes look back at me. Will there be more?

With eyes so wide I dare not blink.

With each footstep my courage does sink.

Into sleep I retreat to escape my fear.

In dreams alone I see my mother most dear.

Dreams untouched end with the onset of light.

A hollow feeling. The absence of night.

My sleep escapes as sound intrudes.

Would be friends seek an interlude.

A new face shines in the light of day.

Cubby seems nice. A friend is made.

The meal was fine. My tummy is filled.

A treasured memory. My heart is stilled.

There's more to be found in this life I call mine.

Treats to be sure. Lots of cuddles so kind.

Oh but of course, Wolfy is here!

The king of the house. The protector from fear.

Later and cuddled, a fort of my own.

A blankie so soft. Some time left alone.

Awakened from dreams of my mama's embrace.

From deep within, here's my grumpiest face.

A sun's warm kiss. With it's light I am touched.

The prettiest of pictures. Not a hair mussed.

So proud, so pretty, so perfect am I!

We calico's are honest. This too. We are not shy!

Mischief be had? Certainly not by me.

I'm keeping myself warm.
Me and my little tootsies.

How'd I get here? What's in the glass?

Does it come out? Oh, how the play time does pass!

Papa, don't look. No, no, go away!

Give me a second. I am only at play!

Help me papa, for I think I am stuck!

Get me down please! I have had some bad luck!

At rest or at play, I am as cute as can be.

For this I know true. Papa always loves me!

Sleep time soon, but I love my new home.

I love my new family and that I'm never alone.

There are many surprises in this home I embrace.

My friends are my family. They bring a smile to my face.

Just one more thought that I give you this day.

Kittens are purr-fect in each and every way!

THE END

Ariel today.

Ariel today.

Made in the USA
Middletown, DE
29 September 2021